Around Royal
Leamington Spa
A Second Selection

IN OLD PHOTOGRAPHS

The former President of the Birmingham Midlands Grocers' Association and the Midlands area of the Retail Fruit Federation, Mr Des Powell, who came to make his home in Leamington from Darlington, thirty-five years ago. He was president twice, 1971–3 and 1984–6.

Around Royal Leamington Spa

A Second Selection

IN OLD PHOTOGRAPHS

JACQUELINE CAMERON

Alan Sutton Publishing Limited
Phoenix Mill · Far Thrupp · Stroud
Gloucestershire

First Published 1994

Dedicated to Bruce and Susan Bell, whose friendship I have enjoyed over the years.

British Library Cataloguing in Publication Data.
A catalogue record for this book is available from
the British Library.

ISBN 0–7509–0702-9

Typeset in 9/10 Sabon.
Typesetting and origination by
Alan Sutton Publishing Limited.
Printed in Great Britain by
The Guernsey Press Company Limited,
Guernsey, Channel Islands.

Contents

This photograph shows the Mayor of Leamington Spa, Alan Dorey, talking to the Plant Manager of the Ford Motor Company, George Jackson, probably in the early 1970s. Alan Dorey now lives in Jersey.

Introduction

Once again I find myself in the delightful position of being asked to compile a second selection of *Around Royal Leamington Spa in Old Photographs*, where not only myself, but more importantly the people of Leamington, have the opportunity to contribute towards the recording of the history of a town we all hold dear to our hearts.

Leamington, despite progress over the years, has still managed to maintain the charisma of yesteryear, thanks mainly to its listed buildings, which form much of the Main Parade, the impressive Victorian Town Hall, the delightful Pump Rooms and the well-maintained Pump Room Gardens and Jephson Gardens, which are a credit to the people who tend them.

To really appreciate the history of Leamington you have to go back to the time when the town was little more than a village with three hundred people living in old cottages, a river prone to flooding that weaved its way around the village and a lifestyle totally different from the one we find today. This village, south of the river, was known as the hamlet of Leamington Priors. It is interesting to observe that by 1783 the hamlet had a church (which for a great many years remained as it was built), the Vicarage, the Mill and Mill House (situated by the River Leam), the Dog and the Old Bowling Green public houses, and the post office (home of Benjamin Satchwell, poet, shoemaker and the town's first postmaster). Along with these there were to be found the old well, the stocks and pound, a duckpond, the village smithy, the poor house, ten pairs of cottages, and three farms with outbuildings, and still with only a population of three hundred.

Things were to change drastically however, with the discovery of the mineral springs in the town, and the ingenuity of two local tradesmen, the inn keeper William Abbotts and cobbler Benjamin Satchwell, mentioned above. For a number of years the two men worked on ways of exploiting the medicinal and financial potential of the waters, in the hope of bringing prosperity and fame to Leamington. It was in 1784 that Dr Kerr of Northampton had called attention to the value of the Leamington waters, and it was upon his advice that the first baths were built in the town. The original baths, opened in 1786, were soon to gain momentum as wealthy visitors began to appreciate the healing potential of the saline waters, and from 1790 onwards the town steadily grew. It was not to last, however, as from 1793 until 1806 very little changed, mainly because of the financing of the war with France and a disastrous harvest in 1799.

Things looked grim for the town for a while but they were soon to change, because between 1806 and 1820 the town flourished, new building took place and the town was divided into two parts, the old town and what is known as the new town. The site of the original hamlet, Leamington Priors, to the south of the river, is still referred to as the 'Old Town' to this day. The New Town arose to the north of the river and consisted of tree-lined avenues and brick-built houses with light wrought-iron balconies and pediments.

It is interesting to observe that before 1800 most of Leamington's townspeople earned their living from the land, but after the discovery of the mineral springs the main employment was in building and allied trades as the town developed and the population boomed.

By 1860, Leamington had grown and the population had reached about seventeen thousand, increasing to around twenty-six thousand by the turn of the century; by 1930 it had increased even further to about thirty thousand.

Alas, this sudden growth brought about the existence of two distinct groups of people in the town. With the cheap and plentiful supply of domestic help, the rich spent their days enjoying lavish shopping sprees on the smart Parade, taking coffee and cakes in the historic Pump Rooms, usually listening to a band, and generally socializing with the élite of the town. In contrast life in the late nineteenth century for the working classes was not so easy. They spent long hours labouring for a small amount of money (an eight-hour day was not generally adopted until 1900), so had very little time for leisure. Behind the façades of the magnificent villas and tree-lined terraces, slums thrived, with as many as two hundred sharing a toilet! This resulted in a large slum clearance programme and the establishment of the Fairweather Fumigation Parlour. The poor lived in back-to-back houses, and their standard of living left much to be desired. Despite this they were a closely knit community, and areas such as Satchwell Park, Queen Street and Tavistock Street, to be found behind the splendour of the new Leamington, were home to a band of happy people, whose social life was simple but enjoyed to the full.

The inevitable happened, and with the availability of cheap labour industrial investment was enticed to the town. Engineering works were established in Leamington along with a number of businesses that enjoyed a worldwide reputation. The town already had a gas supply, which had been brought into the town from Warwick in 1823, the Warwick and Napton Canal opened on 19 March 1800, the railway line from Coventry was completed on 14 December 1844, and electricity came to the town in 1887, so Leamington was well prepared for this industrial invasion.

On the social front Edward Willes, Lord of the Manor, had given land in 1836, and this was laid out in the memory of Dr Jephson. It was known then as Newbold Gardens, and later became the town's famous Jephson Gardens. The tenure of the lease was two thousand years and the rent – a peppercorn – was paid annually. Dr Jephson had been a well-liked and respected practitioner, and began to practise in Leamington as assistant to Dr Chambers, who practised medicine at 11 Union Parade. Dr Jephson was later to have his own practice at 7 York Terrace, where he concentrated on the welfare of the town. Jephson Gardens are a well-known feature of Leamington and do much to enhance the beauty of the town. In the gardens can be seen the Hitchman Fountain, the Corinthian Temple, which houses the statue of Dr Jephson, two fountains in the garden lake, similar in design to those found at Hampton Court, a clock which stands in the centre of the Rose Gardens, and the Willes Obelisk.

In order to cater for the steady growth of the town three bridges were built spanning the River Leam. The first bridge to be constructed was the Leamington Bridge, now known as the Victoria Bridge, which can be found on the main Parade. It was built in 1809, and extended in 1840 and 1848. The erection of the Willes Bridge in 1827 and later the Adelaide Bridge in 1850 made access from the south of the town to the north of the river much easier.

The town took its royal status from a visit by Queen Victoria in 1838, and Leamington (which means 'town on the Leam') became known as Royal Leamington Spa.

As time went by the prosperity of the town increased. Lockheed Automotive Products was founded in Leamington in 1934; Flavell's Gas Appliances was a long established company, and its foundry in Myton Road was purchased in August 1940 by the Ford Motor Company which still occupies the site. The lull that had followed the success of the mineral springs began to disappear as greater employment opportunities were offered by the three main employers.

Several much-needed housing estates were constructed between 1919 and 1930, which improved the housing standards of the town. Family businesses began to spring up. G. Hazell Smith, gents' tailor, was established in 1905 in Regent Street (and still trades there today). E. Francis and Son's, retailer of furniture, materials and clothes, was founded in 1840, and was built on the site of Leamington's second mineral spring. Burgis and Colbourne's, which started life as as a grocer's but grew into a large general store, opened in Bedford Street in 1874.

Over the years Leamington has retained much of its character, mainly because of sensible planning, and the dedication of the people of Leamington, who work together to make sure their town is one to be proud of.

Fast becoming one of the country's most up and coming tourist attractions, the town has much to offer. Its people are warm and friendly, while the Main Parade and the impressive shopping arcades, which now stand where slums and small businesses once thrived, are a constant reminder of the town's prosperity.

I have loved Leamington since I was a child, and the town is still very special to me, which is something I hope I have shared with you through the pages of the book. It has been a pleasure and a privilege to compile this second

SECTION ONE

Let's Open the Album

A Leamington family. Gladys Bench, Doris Reid and baby Carol Anne Reid are pictured in their back garden at Old Milverton, 1950. Old Milverton is about a mile from the centre of Leamington.

A delightful photograph of Doris Favell, who was supervisor of the Post Room at Lockheed Automotive Products from 12 June 1946 until her retirement on 2 June 1961.

Arthur Moss is seen working in his backyard in Moss Street, early 1920s. The baby in the pram is his grandchild.

This delightful photograph was taken in 1940, and shows Mrs Marjorie Ivens holding her goddaughter, Jacqueline Cox, in the back garden. Mrs Ivens still resides in Leamington with her husband George and the little girl grew up to be the present author.

Probably taken in the Ford Motor Company canteen in the mid-1940s, this shows 'Tiny' Murphy, with his hands full. The lovely 'lady' in the straw hat is none other than Larry Grayson, whose stage name at this time was Billy Bean.

Taken in the 1940s during a tea break at the Ford Motor Company, the staff of the Core Shop posed for this photograph in the yard, with the Grafton steam crane visible in the background. The two ladies in the front row are Pat Corley (left) and Irene D'Arcy.

Tony Hoffman junior and Jack O'Donnell enjoying a trip to the Rudesheim wine festival in 1971. Tony Hoffman has raised thousands of pounds for the local hospital's League of Friends.

The Gardner Merchant Food Caterers' 'Ladies' football team. Back row, left to right: Joyce Austin, Pat Hadland, Pat Gorman, -?-, George Smith, Vera Halford. Front row: Vera Lockwood, Mavis Paget, Sandra Brown.

Annie Elizabeth Elswood, *c.* 1920. This photograph was taken in Warwick Castle, where she was employed in service as a cook before her marriage.

Annie (née Elswood) and Joseph George Calcutt, seen here with their youngest son Arthur, 1940. Annie was a Warwick girl who, before her marriage, worked as a cook at both Warwick Castle and the Globe in Warwick. After their marriage they made their home in Joyce Pool, in Leamington. Joseph worked for the Water Board as a plumber and pipe fitter and his youngest son Arthur has followed in the family trade. Joseph and Annie Calcutt had eight children but lost two of them in a diphtheria epidemic which hit the town around 1925.

Arthur Wickes and the family horse, c. 1938. This was used for pulling the cart which carried produce from the family farm. Leamington was once a farming area and as late as the mid-1930s there were many slaughterhouses in the town.

Professor Kevin Cox, 1950s. Professor Cox was educated at nearby Warwick School before taking his degree at Cambridge University. Now Professor of Geography at the State University in Ohio, he is married with two children.

Laurence Kord, 1960. Laurence was born in Northway and educated at St Bede's and Princethorpe College, and was a local junior chess champion. Laurence is now married and lives in Stratford-upon-Avon.

No album would be complete without its lighter moments and here we see Tony Middleton, a janitor, busy planting his spring bulbs in the Ford Motor Company's garden border, 1970s. His labours were to prove in vain, as no blooms appeared that year!

Geoff Clarke is seen here in 1970 proudly displaying a certificate that was presented to him by the Salt Lake City Police Department. Geoff has for many years collected police patches from every state in America.

Mr and Mrs Walter Wickes in the Jephson Gardens with their son Arthur, 1930s. The family is involved with the Royal Antediluvian Order of Buffalos, and was also involved in the Leamington Boy's Club for many years.

Carol Theobald, who swopped her apron strings for a safety helmet to become the country's only female furnace liner and rammer. The furnace is lined along with the spout that feeds the furnace. It gets blocked when the metal freezes and needs dynamite to blow it out. After this, she relines the furnace and rams the spout with a special compound. It is dangerous and filthy work and when Carol is relining the furnace she has to work twenty-four hours as the 'mix' sets quickly.

True dedication is seen here as George Smith, Master Chef at the Gardner Merchant Canteen, goes on a sponsored run for the Myton Hospice Appeal, in the 1980s. A fundraiser for many years, he provided a free dinner and cabaret for 125 pensioners each Christmas.

'After the Lord Mayor's Show', early 1960s. Mrs Liz Bullas is pushing her grandson Rodney away from the sweet pea stall, at the Ford sports ground, Myton Road. The man in the centre is John King, a staff nurse at the local medical centre and seated beneath the umbrella is Hilda Rutkowska. The sweet peas were grown by Alan Williams, who developed the Grace of Monaco and the Leamington varieties.

Little Georgie Warr, aged five, *c*. 1910. Unfortunately he was drowned in an accident a few weeks after the photograph was taken.

The staff and friends of Gardner Merchant Food Caterers, ready to begin their sponsored run for charity, 1980s. Left to right: Brian Clemens and son, Eileen Aston, Jane and her mum Mavis Paget, -?-, -?-, Dot Brown and son, Sandra Brown, George Smith, -?-, Darron Webb, Gemma Wild, Andrew Wild, wearing hat and glasses (the unit manager), Mary Ross's son and daughter-in-law, children and friends.

The man on the left of the front row is Frank Olds, a grocer, who served as an ambulance driver in the First World War, being unfit for active service. The photograph was taken around 1917.

Here we see post-war wedding guests together with bride and groom recording the great day. Back row, left to right: Ron Moss, Edna Williams, -?-, -?-, -?-. Front row: Mrs Williams, Walter Wickes, -?-, Florence Wickes, David Wickes, Vera ?, Ruby Wickes, bridesmaid Doreen ?, -?-, -?-.

Derby Moss at the wheel of a road roller, *c.* 1900. Unfortunately the names of the two men and the little boy are unknown.

Taken in Moss Street in 1935, this delightful photograph shows, left to right: Mrs Wickes, baby David, Mr Elliot, Arthur Wickes, and proud father, Walter Wickes, after the baby's christening.

Old pals enjoying a drink together. Left to right: David Wickes, George Law, Mr Digweed, -?-.

Exchanging a friendly greeting are Bill Shead senior (left) and George Jackson, 1950s. Bill was instrumental in bringing over Irish labour to Leamington after the war. George was the Plant Manager at the Imperial Foundry.

At the annual fête, held on the Ford sports ground, three old friends take the opportunity to have a chat, 1960s. Left to right: Jo Williams (wife of sweet pea grower, Alan), Aubrey Phipps, John Harris, who was a supervisor at the Imperial Foundry laboratory.

Fairs are held in the town throughout the year on the Campion Hills and along the Myton Road. Here we see Hilda Rutkowska deciding whether to try her luck.

SECTION TWO

Into the Twentieth Century

Brunswick Street at the turn of the century, before the days of the motor car, when a little boy could pose relatively safely in the middle of the road.

The Manor House in Avenue Road still looks very much the same as it did when this photograph was taken. Extensions and modifications have made it a much larger building than in 1780, when it was the residence of Matthew Wise. Renowned for its association with lawn tennis, there is a plaque on the lawn which reads 'On this lawn the first Tennis Club in the world was founded in 1872'.

Harry Crawley's tailor's and outfitter's shop traded in the town for many years. It stood on the corner of Regent Street and The Parade, and was known as Logan's before the Second World War.

Nathaniel Hawthorne, the American writer who produced the series of English Sketches in 1863, lived at 10 Lansdowne Circus (above). The Circus and Lansdowne Terrace (below) date back to the 1820s. These line drawings were produced in the late 1940s.

The Hitchman Fountain was built in 1869 as a memorial to Dr Hitchman. He believed in hydropathic treatment and did much to enhance the town's claim to natural medication. In the background can be seen the town's historic Pump Rooms.

This group of handsome men was the police cricket team, seen here before the Second World War, when they were known affectionately as the 'Cricks' and played on a small secluded ground off the Leam Terrace at the back of the Tennis Club. During the war the police cricket team moved its ground to the other side of the river and local spectators would take a raft over the water to watch their favourite players.

The police swimming team, 1943. The gentleman standing third from the right was known as 'Tea Pot Taylor' because of his love of a cup of tea. The man to his right is Ken Smart.

The London Central Meat Company's shop at 14 Clemens Street, c. 1950. The shop closed in 1960, to be replaced the following year by Baxters (Butchers) Ltd. Kwik Save superstore now occupies the site.

The Midland Oak, which was reputed to be the centre of England. This grand tree was chopped down in 1960 and a new one has been planted in the same spot.

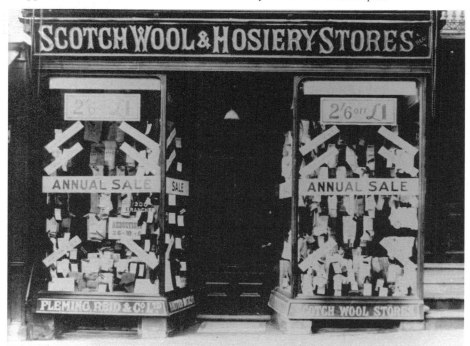

Bellman's Scotch Wool shop at 74 The Parade, early 1970s. The shop is no longer trading.

The lovely Victoria Bridge, which was widened in October 1847 and carries heavy traffic through the town centre daily. The bridge that it replaced was only 23 ft wide; the width between the parapets of the present bridge is 40 ft, though it has recently been narrowed as part of a traffic-calming exercise.

Olds', 1935. The shop was on the corner of Lansdowne Street and Swan Street, opposite the Lansdowne Tavern, which was known as the Butcher's Arms at the time.

I can well recall walking through this department of E. Francis and Son in Bath Street when I was a young girl. It was spacious, the blouses were lovely, and the staff were keen to help. Unfortunately the business closed in 1983, to be replaced by Tandy.

The Leamington gas works at Ranleigh Terrace, c. 1935.

Victoria Terrace seen from the parish church, 1930s, in the days when there was a lawn at the entrance to the church, and beautiful wrought-iron railings were the order of the day.

Looking up The Parade, the building on the left is the famous Pump Rooms. On the right is the Jephson Gardens.

Rossmore House in Newbold Terrace was built in the 1840s and was renovated in 1985 by A.C. Lloyd (Builders) Limited, which won a prestigious award for its efforts. This photograph shows the building before its restoration. The house now forms part of a large business complex.

Bailey's furniture store served the town for many years in Warwick Street, until September 1992, when it fell casualty to the recession. It was a family business concentrating mainly on exclusive furniture, although in its early days perambulators, such as the elegant Silver Cross, were sold. Before ceasing to trade, the business had become a franchise. BeWise now occupies the site.

SECTION THREE

In Service to the Town

Trying out his skill at the controls of a Stacka truck is Frederick Isaac Eaton, who was the Mayor of Leamington Spa from 1963 to 1964. The man second from the left is Tony Rayment and second from the right is Albert McCartney.

Mrs Phyllis Key, a popular local lady who took a keen and active interest in public life. She was married to Sid and had three sons, two of whom still live locally. During the war she became a street collector for the National Savings Scheme and went on to complete twenty-five years' service. A keen supporter of the Women's Conservative Association, she stood as a candidate for the Brunswick Ward for many years. She was also a keen fundraiser for the RNLI. Phyllis received an invitation to a garden party at Buckingham Palace in July 1966, in recognition of her efforts for the National Savings Scheme. This took place just two days before Phyllis' death.

A mayoral visit to the Ford Motor Company in 1954. Photographed walking along the Myton Road, the group is observing a modernization programme on the south front by Turriff's of Warwick. The group includes Dr Croft (left), George Jackson (second from left) and Rolly Wood (right).

There is nothing like a good laugh and here we see the Women's Conservative Association Chairman, Mrs Wood, doing just that, in 1960.

The ABA Midland Area Middleweight Champion, Willie Stack, after his comfortable win over R. Barber, of Wilmot Breedon. Fighting his way through three fights on Saturday 22 February 1964, Willie then set his sights on the All England ABA Middleweight Championships, to be fought at a later date in Birmingham. A place in the Olympic Team in Tokyo rested on the final results of this competition. Willie went to Tokyo, but unfortunately he did not win.

The Top Firm for 1973 in a local competition was the Ford Motor Company. Left to right: Sid Foster, Phil McKeown, -?-, -?-, Phil Stanley, Barbara Green, -?-, Mr Hopkins (Mayor), -?-.

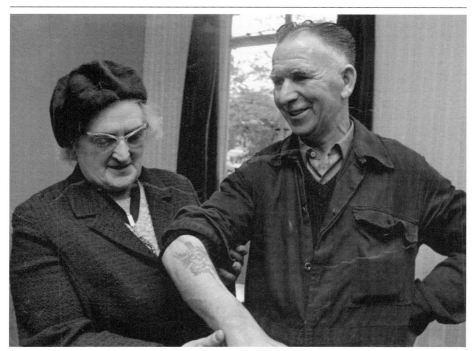

If you have got it flaunt it and Wally Herbert is doing just that, showing Mayor Irene Randall his tattoo during a visit to a local factory! Irene was mayor in 1968/9.

Hammick's Bookshop, whose dynamic manager Philip Bonehill does much to promote Leamington's local history. The shop has now moved into much larger premises on the second floor of the Priors Mall Shopping Centre.

Local MP Anthony Eden trying out for himself the wonders of modernization – a farm component made at the Ford Motor Company. Eden was the MP from 1923 to 1957.

This postcard, *c.* 1907, shows one of the trams that served the town for many years before the motor car. The statue of Queen Victoria seen outside the Town Hall was placed there in 1902, with a paved area and small garden around it.

A rare photograph taken during the town's Golden Jubilee celebrations in 1934.

West End Garage, 1950s. It is still in business.

Ready for the road! This bus has a Tilling engine, and the driver is John Cambray.

Patricia P. Robinson was Mayor in 1984. Born in Portsmouth, Pat and her husband made Leamington their home in 1955, two years after their marriage. In the mid-1960s she became actively involved in local politics and eventually became an elected member of the Leamington Borough Council. Local government re-organization meant that as a member of Warwick District Council representing Kingsway Ward Pat automatically became a Charter Trustee. A teacher of needlecraft for Warwick County Council, she was to change departments in 1977, when she joined the Social Services in a day centre for people with learning difficulties. A governor of Lillington Middle School for many years, Pat is currently a member of the governing body of Round Oak School and Chairman of the Governers at Lillington Nursery School. Both Pat and her husband actively support town twinning. Pat has been a member of the Leamington in Bloom committee for many years. She has a son and a daughter.

Leamington Spa's only known windmill, which gave its name to the public house in Tachbrook Road. It had its sails removed in 1943, and was completely demolished in 1968. It is pictured at the turn of the century.

This pair of wedding cars was captured on film waiting for a wedding party from St Mary's Church, *c.* 1947. They were owned by Mr Chamberlain, the proprietor of West End Garage. His widow now runs the business.

SECTION FOUR

Peeps into the Past

Ready for action. This fire engine and ambulance were called to the fire at the Shakespeare Memorial Theatre, Stratford-upon-Avon in 1926.

Photographed early this century, this delightful group of children attended the Clapham School in Clapham Terrace.

This tranquil scene of The Parade from Victoria Bridge in 1906 contrasts strangely with the traffic congestion today. In October 1823 eighteen lamps were erected along The Parade, and were lit by a gas company in Warwick. The mains were laid from Warwick in July 1823 and were financed by the residents on The Parade, who had to pay a substantial amount per annum for the privilege.

Reputed to be the finest of their type in the country, the Pump Rooms cost £30,000 to build. Designed by Mr C.S. Smith of Warwick, they were opened in July 1814, and were open daily from 7 a.m. until 3 p.m., except during the time of divine service. The Pump Rooms were built for a syndicate comprising Mr B.B. Greatheed of Guys Cliffe, Mr Tomes (the banker), Mr Parkes and Mr H.W. Tancred, both of Warwick.

This photograph, taken from the Victoria Bridge in the early 1900s, looks towards Bath Street, and shows the cabmen's hut on the left, the Aylesford Well in the centre of the picture and Victoria Terrace on the right.

An early picture of The Parade, taken *c*. 1910, before the days of the motor car.

These fine examples of the town's wrought-iron work are the main gates to the Jephson Gardens, seen here in the early 1950s. On either side of them can be found a picturesque lodge. The north side gate has a small bronze shield which bears the Borough's coat of arms, with the following inscription: 'These gates were presented by Rowland Sydney Salt, Chairman of the Parks and Gardens Committee 1948.' On the south side gate is fixed a shield bearing a large Borough coat of arms on the front and the following inscription on the back: 'Borough of Royal Leamington Spa. Jephson Gardens opened in 1846.'

This delightful little lake can be found by the Mill Gardens, where its tranquillity can still be enjoyed to this day. The wrought-iron work and rustic bridge enhance the beauty of the picture, taken in 1900.

Walter Wickes, member of the Royal Antediluvian Order of Buffalos, is pictured here in 1920.

George Charles Warr of Leam Terrace in his allotment, showing how to grow a good onion. George won first, second and third prizes with his onions as a member of the Leamington St Mary's General Onion Growers Association. The rule of entry was that the crop had to be grown on the St Mary's allotments in Radford Road. Incidentally George's onions were grown on allotments with no water supply.

Keeping the spirits high in the 1940s! Seen here 'rolling the barrel' is Tommy Trinder, who was captured on film during a visit to Lockheed Automotive Products.

The Cycling and Athletic Club, Pump Rooms, mid-1920s. George Davies is on the left of the back row, and centre of the row in front is Sidney Wild.

Hortence Ballard, or Gheil as she was known, served her apprenticeship with E. Francis and Son before 1923. She later married Frank Olds, and is seen here with her daughter Josephine.

A.C. Lloyd's yard in Camberwell Terrace. The business was established in the town in 1946. Cyril Lloyd, carpenter and joiner, was the founder of A.C. Lloyd's (Builders) Ltd, which has since won numerous awards for design and building skills in the area.

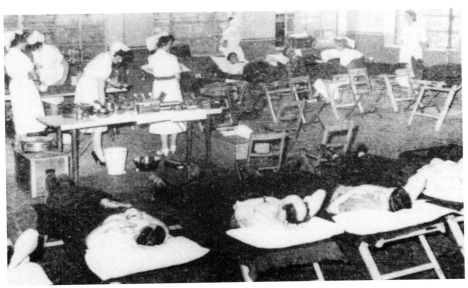

The first visit of the National Blood Transfusion Group to the Imperial Foundry was made in July 1958. It was a very casual affair by today's standards, for as soon as the main lunch break had finished at 1.30 p.m. all the tables and chairs were removed from the canteen, which was handed over to the Transfusion Group fifteen minutes later. At 2.45 p.m. the first eight volunteers were accepted, with further batches of eight at fifteen minute intervals until 4.45 p.m. The unit was then cleared up by 6 p.m.

Seen here in the mid-1950s enjoying a well-earned holiday is Billy Pugh, a local council worker, who lived in Buckley Road.

These lovely ladies are, from left to right: Winnie Bell, Margret Bell (her mother-in-law), Eleanor Storey and Mrs Bell, who was visiting from Blyth in northern England, 1930s.

SECTION FIVE

The Changing Face
of Leamington

Pierre Picton, the international clown, entertaining a group of local children, 1970s. The little boy in the centre is Adrian Cowley.

A presentation to Ernest Bradford, builder, on his golden wedding, *c.* 1963. Back row, left to right: -?-, George Wrighton, Monty Plummer, Mr Lock, -?-, Rod Blyth, Tom Nicholson, Les Meredith, Harry Warr, -?-, Bill Sharpe. Front row: Bert Tandy, John Bradford, Ernest Bradford, Ernest Bradford junior, Bill Humphries.

Taken at the retirement of John Everitt, who worked for Ford Motor Company during the 1980s. His former colleagues sit with him in the Nelson Hall for this delightful photograph. Left to right: John Faringdon, Liz Bullas, Kath Green, Sid Thornton, Willie Green, John Everitt, Reg Hunt.

Bruce Bell, Plant Manager of the Ford Motor Company, presents a carriage clock to Val Andrews, who for many years waited at the manager's table in the manager's dining room at Ford's, for Gardner Merchant Catering.

The Ford Motor Company office cricket team, early 1970s. Standing, left to right: Mel Moore (umpire), Eric Kennell, Tom Jennings, Frank Flynn, Alan Hassall, Phil Leeson, Sid Thornton, Fred Goodchild. Seated: Dave Wood, Mike Callaghan, Brian Smith, Glyn Morgan.

A tranquil scene of Leamington Old Town greets you from the windows of the Grand Union Restaurant, which is the brainchild of Eric Shadbolt, seen here. This lovely corner of Leamington draws diners from all over the world. At 8 o'clock sharp the gong sounds as a signal for everyone to sit down at their tables, and a resumé of how the evening will run is given by Eric and his manager, David Nicholl. The diners have a six course meal ahead of them, including the famous Pudding Parade when up to nine different sweets are paraded before each table. In all its thirteen years in business the Grand Union has never advertised. Currently the building on the right of the picture, which is also owned by Eric, is being converted into a private hotel.

Employees of the Imperial Foundry. From left to right: Jackie Kord, Liz Bullas and Ron and Heather Chisholm enjoying the fun of the fête on a breezy day in the early 1970s.

The blind bowlers of Leamington met at Victoria Park every Wednesday morning. The man fourth from the right is Bill Wilson, who was in charge.

The works dinner was very popular in the 1950s and '60s. Here we see Jimmy Hill (left), with Ron Isham beside him; the woman on the right is Mrs Hill.

Mr and Mrs David Wickes on their wedding day.

SECTION SIX
A Town at Work

Henry Lesnik came to England after the Second World War from his native Poland to make his home in Leamington. One of a large community of Polish residents, Henry was the last Polish employee to leave the Ford Motor Company when he retired in July 1990.

From left to right: Ken Harman, Neil McCall, Chris McCann and Andrew Bean of ICS – one of the contracting companies which operate in the town.

The Grafton steam crane, which belonged to the Imperial Foundry, 1940s. It could be seen operating in Myton Road for many years.

Workers' playtime at the Imperial Foundry in the early 1960s. The man in the centre of the photograph in glasses is Vince Malone. Also here are Johny Mulcahy, Maurice Malone, Jack Bissell and John Hargrave.

Midland-born Bruce Bell, the Plant Manager of the Ford Motor Company.

Edith Warr, seen here in 1924, by the annexe wall at the Pump Rooms where she worked as a waitress. The tea rooms were open all year (except for Christmas Day) from 9 a.m. until 7 or 7.30 p.m.

Len Dillow (in the trilby hat) supervising the moving of a linotype machine, for typesetting, from the old Courier Press works in Bedford Street to the new premises in Tachbrook Road. He was a local haulier, who ran a business in the town in the 1950s.

John Jarratt showing off his prize beasts, with the help of two of his sons, *c.* 1937.

Elm Farm Dairy Company Ltd, Regent Street, *c.* 1900. Pure new milk was sold from their carts.

Mr and Mrs Dick Hatton (on the left), and Mr and Mrs Don Rutherford at a Christmas party, early 1970s. Don was Plant Manager at the Imperial Foundry, and Dick worked there all his life. The Hattons organized this annual party.

From left to right: Den Burridge, John Miley, Sam Barriscale, -?-, Ernie Murray and 'Mac' Macintyre at a business lunch, mid-1960s.

A leaving presentation to Mr Thursfield, a safety officer at the Imperial Foundry. From left to right: Edgar Evans, John Moore, Jim Butcher, Bob Attwood, Sam Barriscale, Joan Smith, 'Tiny' Murphy, David Chase, Ann Giles, Ces Mullard, Chris Tew, Mr Thursfield, John Harris, Bill Edwards and Charlie Stratton.

An outing to Clacton for the works staff of Henry Griffiths and Son's jewel factory, Tachbrook Road (now MCR Motors), 1959 or 1960. The photograph was taken before their departure on the day trip. Back row, left to right: Derek Horley, Ken Walters, Marie ?, Shirley Handy, Bet Billington, -?-, Pauline Lecocq, -?-, Ethel Harris. Front row: Carol Billington, Nora Heeler, Vi Holt, Maureen Billington, Janet ?, Jackie Clarke, -?-, Barbara Corefield, -?-, Eileen Day. The two people kneeling are Betty Faries and Daphne Clarke.

A presentation to employees for long service to the Ford Motor Company. Back row, left to right: Ron Williams, Den Burridge, ? Flynn, John Moore, Don Brown, Bruce Bell. Front row, left to right: Stan Grenway, Geoff Gardner, Ron Checkley.

Jackie Kord, Secretary to the Finance Manager of the Ford Motor Company, 1974.

Jim King (in the cap) on his retirement from the Ford Motor Company receiving his retirement present from Frank Herbert of Estates and Buildings, 1960s. From left to right: Albert Crosbee, Mick Wrestley, Frank Farrell, -?-, -?-, Jim Murphy, John Hannan, G. Wilson, Harry McGreever, Jack O'Donnell, Martin Gleeson, Ted Parker and 'Jukie'.

Photographed in 1948, these four shorthand typists were employed at Lockheed Automotive Products in the shorthand room. Back row, left to right: Rhona Bayliss, Anne Oliver. Front row: Doris Sharman, Helen Hurst.

The works canteen at the Ford Motor Company, early 1950s. The man on the right with the moustache is John Whitmore. Though he retired many years ago, he is now a pensioners' visitor for the company.

A retirement presentation to Kath Green from the Plant Controller, Phil Davidson, early 1970s. Also pictured from left to right: Frank Wall (of Wall's Roses fame), Alan Williams, Willy Green, Pam Willes, Ernie Bateman, Liz Bullas, Tony Pomfret (taller of the two men in glasses), Aubrey Phipps.

HM Queen Elizabeth the Queen Mother visited Lockheed Automotive Products in Tachbrook Road on Thursday 6 November 1958.

Break-time on the moulding lines at the Ford Motor Company.

In the ballroom at Lockheed Automotive Products, 1959. From left to right: George Elliot (General Secretary), Joyce Mason (Sports and Social Club Secretary), Doris Favel (Sports and Social Club Committee Member), J. Smith (Chairman of AP Sports and Social Club).

On the farm in Myton Road. Now on this site is a shopping complex.

The works dinner at the Ford Motor Company, early 1970s. Back row, left to right: Vince Malone, -?-, -?-, Derek Hunt, Alan Thompson ,-?-, Jock ?, -?-, Percy Ward, Charlie Aston, Bill Edwards, -?-, Charlie Eaton. Seated: Tommy Morgan, Ivor Whitlock, Ockie Holt, -?-, Tommy Barriscale.

They Chose Leamington

Larry Granelly, pictured in 1980. With his wife Terrie and two children he moved from South Wales to Leamington. Larry Granelly is the Area Manager at the Ford Motor Company.

Many families came to make their home in Leamington in the early 1960s. Hari Singh Sohal and his wife Surjit Kaur Sohal arrived with their children, Santokh and Jaswinder Singh, from the Punjab in India. Living in Whitnash Road, Hari found work with the Ford Motor Company and Surjit was to have another son, Amarjit Singh. The children are now grown up and their jobs range from quality controller to chartered accountant and computer scientist.

Andrew Urquart Reid came down from Scotland to marry a local girl, Doris Bench. They are seen here at their wedding in 1944. Also pictured are Gladys and Harry Bench. The couple were to make their home in Old Milverton.

Party Time

Party spirit in the 1950s at the Ford Motor Company. Back row, left to right: Roy Harding, -?-, -?-, -?-, Ken Hydon, -?-, Pat Green, Willy Green, John Everitt, Betty Everitt, Sid Thornton. Middle row: Jim Butcher, Mrs K. Hydon, -?-, -?-, Bill Shead, John Moore, Jo Olds, -?-, Colin Haywood. Front row: -?-, -?-, Fred Goodchild, Frank Wall.

The ladies of the typing pool and the shorthand typists enjoy their Christmas party in the Lockheed Hydraulic Brake Company's ballroom, mid-1940s.

Celebrating retirement from the Ford Motor Company. The party was held at Manor House Hotel, Avenue Road, mid-1970s. Left to right: Geoff Gardner, Ron Bowdidge (Plant Manager and host for the evening), Mrs Gardner, John Faringdon, his wife Vera, -?-, -?-, Mr Tony Hoffman senior, Mrs Hoffman, -?-, -?-, -?-, Ces Manley, -?-, Walter Cobb, Mrs Cobb.

The Pop Art stall at a typical summer fête in the early 1970s.

Enjoying the Christmas festivities at a local Ford Motor Company pensioners reunion party in the early 1980s are, left to right: Mr and Mrs Seeley, Jacqueline Cameron, Jimmy Bartlett and his wife.

Liz Bullas, a Comptometer operator at the Ford Motor Company, arriving with her entry for the cake competition at the works fête in the early 1960s.

In the 1970s carnivals were heralded as a momentous occasion, and all the local industries would enter a float in the hope of gaining the coveted award. Ford's entry is seen here. The two ladies are Linda ? and her cousin. Joe Vaughan is the driver with the crash helmet and goggles. The maintenance crew are Stan Talbot, Derek Witnall, Tony Hoffman junior and Peter Jeffreys.

This photograph is believed to have been taken in Mr Bill Higgins' back garden in Duke Street, 1950s. Enjoying the sunshine are, left to right: Mr and Mrs Frank Herbert, -?-, Mrs Higgins, Bill Higgins.

Bottoms up! Back row, left to right: Tommy Dowling, Dougie Stephens, Roy Harding, -?-, Len Smallwood, David Davies, -?-, Alan Williams, -?-, -?-, -?-. Middle row: -?-, Ken Sharpe, Sid Thornton, -?- , -?-, Hattie Towers, Edgar Evans. Front row: -?-, -?-, Betty Everitt.

Enjoying a drink and a meal are, from left to right: Frank Herbert, -?-, -?-, Ken Sharpe and Tommy Streeter, 1960s.

Dot Brown, on the left of the photograph, can be seen pulling a cracker with Mary Ross at the Gardner Merchant Christmas party, 1980. Looking on in the back row, left to right: Sandra Brown (Dot's sister), Darron Webb (master chef), Barbara Bridge, Kath ?.

This picture was taken outside the sports pavilion in Myton Road, at a retirement party, 1970s. From left to right: -?-, Bill Sturley, -?-, -?-, -?-, -?-, Phil Stanley, 'Lofty' Jukes, Bob Agg, Bill Shead, -?-, John Murphy, Sid Maskell, Trevor Meinert, Mrs Meinert, -?-, -?-, -?-, -?-, -?-, -?-, David Wickes, -?-, George Wesson, Ken Cheshire, -?-, John Whitmore, Bill Davis, Mrs Davis, Bob Attwood, Mrs Attwood.

Members of Leamington Cycling and Athletic Club, 1928. The man in the plus fours is Sid Wild.

Lockheed staff works dinner, the ballroom, 1940s.

These lovely children were photographed at Clapham Terrace School in 1952. The little girl sitting down third from the left is Irene Barlow, the third little boy standing from the left is Godfrey Barker and the little boy standing second from the right is Jeffrey Wickes, who was sadly killed in an accident some years later.

The Parade, 1929. Granny Olds is seen pushing the pram. The little girl on the left is Brenda Olds, the little boy in the middle is Alan Brentnal, and Pat Olds is on the right.

The summer fête, held on the Imperial Foundry sports ground. Seen here are Colin Haywood, Mike Massey and Brenda Massey.

Enjoying a pint at a works dinner in the Ford Sports and Social Club, early 1970s. The photograph includes Arthur Arrowsmith (front left), Billy Lees (behind), Percy 'the Greaser' (front right), Freddy Humphries (behind, in glasses), George Cleaver (back table, right) and Frank Fennell (to his right).

Photographed in the mid-1960s are, from left to right: Ernie Bateman, Mrs Bateman, -?-, -?-, 'Taffy' Williams, Mrs Williams. The occasion is unknown.

In the 1950s the children's Christmas party was part of the Imperial Foundry's calendar year, and great effort was put in by staff to ensure the children had a good time. Judging by the look on the little girl's face, they had the right ingredients. Serving the food is Ted Green.

Lockheed staff party, early 1940s. This took place each year in the staff canteen.

Father Christmas arriving for the children's party at the Ford Motor Company, 1960s. Left to right: Colin Haywood, Mick Daly, David Wickes, Father Christmas, Mrs Dick Hatton, -?-, -?-, -?-.

The Round Table 'It's a Knock Out' competition, in which works teams competed for a cup. The two ladies facing the camera are Eileen and Barbara Green, *c.* 1970.

'Signs of the Zodiac', the Ford entry in an early 1970s carnival, won first prize. From left to right: Ken Pearcy, Phil Stanley, Bill ?, Sid Foster, John Whitmore, Brian Smith, Dave Wickes, Pete Jeffreys, John Everitt, Glyn Morgan, Henry ?, Joe Vaughan, Tommy Jennings, Derek Toone, Tony Hoffman junior, and their young lady helpers.

Firework display on 5 November in the late 1960s. Guests for the evening were the Sealed Knot, and the venue was the Ford Motor Company car park. The man in the check jacket is Tony Hoffman junior.

Eadie and Harry Warr of Leam Terrace taking part in the 1937 Prosser Trials in north Devon. Harry ran a building, decorating and plumbing business in Leamington.

The 1958 Taj Mahal Goodwill Coach Tour from Leamington to India was the fulfilment of a dream for the proprietor of West End Garage, Ken Chamberlain. An Indian gentleman called into his office asking for a quotation for driving a coach a few thousand miles – Leamington to India, halfway round the world – and back again. Mr Chamberlain is seen on the far right.

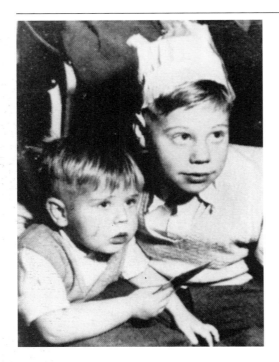

These two little ones were photographed at a Christmas party, given by the Imperial Foundry, in the early 1950s.

Joe Davies, the Core Shop clerk and trainer of the Ford Football Team, puts the players through their paces on the sports ground in 1956.

The Campion School play, 1934.

Singing on stage. Children enjoy a Christmas party at the Imperial Foundry, early 1950s.

'I'm telling you it's real cream!' Children of Ford Motor Company employees enjoy a Christmas party, held in the Gardner Merchant Canteen in the early 1970s.

SECTION NINE

The Town's Achievements

The occasion is unknown, but it was probably at the Imperial Foundry, in the late 1960s. The group includes Dougie Stevens (back row, second from right) and his wife Betty (front row, second from right).

Seen here in 1950 is Sir Anthony Eden (centre), who was MP for Leamington for a number of years.

The mayor's annual visit to the Imperial Foundry, 1966. The mayor is Leslie Lionel Freeman.

A visit to the Imperial Foundry, 1950. Names unknown.

This lovely building in Clemens Street started life in 1816 when it was a Nonconformist chapel. By 1848 it had become a theatre, but this was short lived and by 1868 it had become a Congregational Free Church again. It was to become the Zephyr Carburettor Company around 1910, before being used by Lockheed Automotive Products.

The Polishing and Grinding Shop at Sidney Flavel and Co. Ltd, 1930s.

The shop floor at Sidney Flavel and Co. Ltd, 1930s.

The Automotive Block at Lockheed Automotive Products under construction, 1936. The building was to be known as Block Five.

SECTION TEN
People and Places

Edith Warr, Lieutenant of the 10th Leamington Guides. Aged just sixteen, she was the youngest Guide Lieutenant in the world.

Waiting for the Queen Mother's visit to Lockheed Automotive Products in 1958.

Father Christmas delivering the goods at the Ford Motor Company children's party in 1954.

A Leamington family group: Frank and Hortence Olds with their children, *c.* 1929. The children, left to right, are Denis, Pat and Brenda. Frank was in business in the town for many years.

This group was known as the Twenty-Five Club as they were all employees with over twenty-five years' service with Lockheed. The lady third from the right in the front row is Miss Jessie Bishop, who for many years ran the typing pool at the Lockheed works with a rod of iron. Miss Bishop was originally from the London area, but was evacuated to Leamington during the Second World War.

Patch, photographed in 1916, holds happy memories for his owner, Arthur Wickes.

Reg Warr (left) was a well-known Leamington swimmer. This picture, taken in the family garden, also includes his father, George Warr, his mother (name unknown), Mick, Len and his sister Doris.

A ride on the wild side! This intrepid cyclist is pictured on The Parade, opposite the Town Hall, late 1940s. Although the volume of traffic at that time was considerably less than today, large cars could be driven without a test.

Taken on 7 August 1922, this shows a party of people being taken to Cheddar Gorge. The smallest of the two men standing up is Frank Olds.

Marks and Spencer. The date of this picture is unknown, but a very much larger branch stands on this site today.

Enjoying a drink at the Avon Tavern are Tom Cox (left) and friends. Tom is the President of the Oddfellows, Leamington, and he ran his own plastering business in the town before his retirement.

SECTION ELEVEN
Around the Area

This tranquil scene is near Warwick Castle and shows the River Avon, 1920s. The man standing in the boat is Samuel Bissell, who worked the ferry.

Tom Cox proudly holding the Dominoes Cup, which has been won many times by the Avon Tavern.

The Corn Exchange, Warwick. Woolworths took over the building, which was later demolished together with the house on the right. A new Woolworths was erected on the site.

Guy's Cliff Mill.

This tranquil scene is Castle Lane, 1920s. the building on the left is Okens House, which is home of Warwick's famous Doll's Museum.

The ladies of the cigar factory, which traded on Castle Hill before the Second World War, are seen here in the late 1920s.

The Gold Cup in Castle Lane. The building in the centre of the photograph is the Dolls' Museum.

Jackie Cox from Warwick (daughter of Mr and Mrs Cox, below) and Beckie the dog photographed near the Warwick Canal in 1954.

A family group on the doorstep of 78 Hanworth Road. Left to right: Mrs Gillian Webb, her mother and father (Mr and Mrs Jack Cox), Jack's younger brother (Tom Cox).

The Avon Rovers Football Club, 1910.

Delightfully situated on the banks of the River Avon, the Church of the Assumption of Our Lady, Ashow, is renowned for the panelling in the chancel; it also has an old Dutch painting of the Crucifixion over the altar. The date of the church is uncertain owing mainly to the actions of the former parish clerk, who was a publican. It is said that he cut up the earliest volumes of the church register to use as pipe lighters. Consequently the register dates only from 1733. In the churchyard is a yew tree which is estimated to be 386 years old.

The bridge which crosses the Avon. Beyond can be found Bericote Farm, former home of Mrs Hiorns, and the only working farm still in business in a once thriving farming community. The path crosses the abandoned track which served the now deserted village of Bericote. The cottages were built in late nineteenth century in Victorian mock-Tudor style.

Old Cottages, Ashow, *c.* 1910. These would certainly have been connected with agriculture, which was the main source of revenue in the area. Rye and oats were the principal crops.

The dance to select the Cubbington Carnival Queen, 1950s. Back row, left to right: Andrew Wild, Gus Peppitt, Mrs Cowley, Sid Wild, Sheila Cowley, 'Hammer' Lane. Front row: Ada Butler, Edith Andrews, Queenie Hall, Eva Busby, Marge Grant. The little boy sitting at the front is unknown.

Cubbington Albion Football Club, late 1940s. Back row, left to right: Sid Henstone, Dick Heath, Roy Draper, Harry Goddard, Ken Plank, Frank Hughes, John Auston. Front row: Arthur Chamberlain, 'Pim', -?-, Harold Kerry, Len Lambert.

The marshalling team in Warwick, 1950s. They were recording the road races for the Leamington C&ACC. At the back is Sid Wild; in the front row, from left to right are Nancy Adkins, Nora Adkins, -?-, -?-.

Waiting to ring in the new year at Cubbington Church, early 1950s. From left to right: Spencer Hinks, Arthur Hickman, Alan Rose, Walter Levey, Ernest Taylor.

Cubbington May Queen, 1935 or 1936. She is seen here with her attendants outside the vicarage door. Back row, left to right: Marjorie Ward, Kath Nickson, Molly Ward. (The Ward girls are twins.) Front row: -?-, Rita Skelsey, Jean Knight, Audrey Skelsey, Evelyn Proffit.

The Cubbington allotment dinner in the village hall, late 1940s. This was organized by the Allotment Association Committee.

Cubbington Carnival, 1950s. Mr Lines is holding the whistle. 'Hammer' Lane is wearing the school cap. Edith Andrews and Gus Peppitt (school master) are also in the photograph.

Cubbington allotment dinner in the early 1950s.

Cubbington Carnival, in the early 1950s. Back row, left to right: 'Hammer' Lane, Marge Grant, -?-. Front row: Mr Dennis, Winnie Payne, Walter Andrews, Alan Hall, Eve Busby, Miss Denis, Sid Wild (in the mask), Queenie Hall, Bill Richardson.

The Cubbington WI choir before singing at the Musical Festival in the old pavilion in the Jephson Gardens, 1950. Back row, left to right: Bonnie Lambert, Alice Brook, Gladys Duggins, Gwen Williams, Florrie Chamberlain, Barry Timms, Win Cleaver, Mrs Ashton. Middle row: Jill Adkins, Mrs Lloyd, Mrs Brookes, Edie Peppitt, Edith Andrews, Olly Gilbert, Lizzie Stanley, Mrs Harris. Front row: Doris Lambert, Nancy Wild, Nora Box, Nesta Davies, May Bolin, Donald Harris (conductor).

Mick Bench aged three, 1936. The picture was taken at Mackenzie's Farm on the Radford Road. Mr Mackenzie, known as 'Old Mac', also kept Red House pub for many years. As he grew up Mick learned to milk the cows and he also helped Old Mac on his milkround.

Mrs 'Gerty' Nickson was a well-known character in the village. She is seen here with Alan Williams, a family friend, at her granddaughter Linda's wedding at Cubbington Church. The man in the glasses (on Gerty's right) is Tom Nickson, and the man with the receding hair on the left is his son, John Nickson. Mrs Nickson moved from rooms in Lansdown Circus to Church Terrace, Cubbington, in the early 1930s. In 1940 she rented property in the terrace, which was 2s 6d a week. When Gerty moved into Church Terrace, she took the lino from Lansdowne Circus on her bicycle. Her daughter Kath, who was eight years old at the time, still lives in the terrace.

Weston under Wetherly fête, late 1950s. Bob Timms was the checker and the caller was Sid Wild.

The top lock at Hatton, known as the upper wharf. It was on the Warwick to Birmingham Canal and opened in 1793.

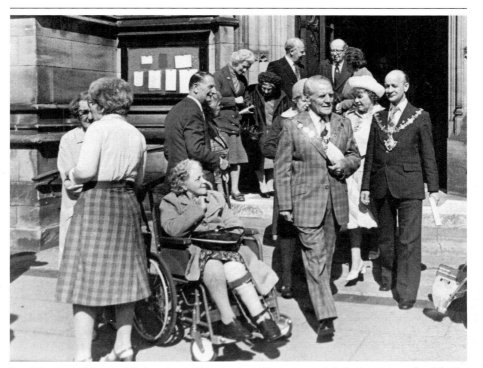

Les Haynes, Mayor of Southam (in check suit, centre right), is pictured with Dr Geoffrey Leese, Mayor of Stratford-upon-Avon (right), and his wife (behind, right).

Acknowledgements

Special thanks go to the following:
Graham Wilton • Geoff Parker • Ann Benninger • Joyce Mason
Mr and Mrs George Ivens • Andrew and Janet Wild • Tony Hoffman senior
Colin Haywood • Warwick Record Office • Leamington Spa Art Gallery
John Victory • Angela Ford • Mr Riman • Mrs Rogers • Mr Geoff Clarke